Maria Andreas

The Tenth Plague

Originally published in French as *La Dixième Plaie*.
Translated into English by Jacqueline Tobin.

First Edition
Huge Jam, 2021

Copyright © 2021 Maria Andreas
First published in English by Huge Jam, 2021.
All rights reserved.
ISBN: 978-1-911249-62-7

Dedication

To all those who have made it possible
for lives to be saved
and suffering to be accompanied.

Preface

THIS PRIVATE JOURNAL runs from March 4th to May 28th, 2020.

As with any diary, its writing springs from an emotion. That very female urge, prompted by the soul's catharsis![1]

Emotion caused sometimes by a personal event, sometimes by a news event. Mostly by the daily news, but sometimes also by intimate memories that such news revived.

It has no medical, political, social, psychological or theological pretensions,

It is content to be a real-life voice of fire, during a period of undeniably historic upheaval.

---

[1] Katharos in Greek means: pure. Originally these purists rejected the world created by evil. They belonged to an early 13th century cult, especially in the southwest of France.

This voice is above all that of a Christian, who questions her God about what she has called: "The Tenth Plague", referring to the book of Exodus.

Maria Andreas does not assume that she has received an answer. She remains alert and lucid. Authentic too. And it is in this authenticity, as well as in her memories and her intimate dialogue with The Christ, that she draws elements of comfort, beyond the boundaries of the church and, even more so, beyond those of an arrogant morality.

Thus resounds this "question-answer" supplication about the deceased who arrive before the door of paradise:

"But I am sure, if they ask You:
Let them be called, Jimmy, Inaya, Diego, Isaac, Assad, Esther, Liang, Daisy, Moussa, Arun, Tom…
Or even Jojo…
If they ask YOU …
You will open the door for them.
Because *La Tendresse*[2]:
It's YOU!"

*"Thank you for the roses,
thank you for the thorns!"*[3]

---

[2] Tenderness, see p 40 of this book
[3] Jean D'Ormesson

'Le Journal'

March 4, 2020

So light

    Nature is trampling.
    Lightly.
    On the lookout, ready to catch fire at the sun's slightest provocation.
    And he, the little Minus?
    Nanometer[4] so light in nature.
    Is he on the lookout, too?
    The evil little Minus has not yet reached the city.
    In this provincial city in Switzerland, local radio only reported a first case on February 28th.

---

[4] One millionth of a millimetre

A young woman, returned from a trip to Milan.

Milan, where hell opened its doors to him, to the evil little Minus.

It's certain that they are colluding!

Milan... It's far away.

And China, despite globalisation, is even further.

On 1st March however, two groups were quarantined.

What is quarantine?

Originally around 1180, it was the period of the Great Lent[5].

40 days to turn yourself around.

Return to Your Creator.

Return to your heart.

And towards your body, shaking it up.

Signifying to it, that it is not the only master on board.

Turning yourself around to face... all your shit:

Like that of adopting an indifferent compassion, since Milan is far away and China further still, and since hell was in the Middle Ages!

And as for the Creator, we can go party with Him with our imperial science and our ingenious computers!

Without which I could neither write nor communicate.

---

[5] 40 days to prepare for the Passover, to give the body lean food and to the soul, more meditation. The sense of measuring health dates back to the 14th century.

So, this is not the time to be bothering ourselves with quarantine!

No but!

March 5, 2020

Sparks of laughter

I am grateful.

Facing the window.

That recognises me.

Lying on one of the beds in the small oncology clinic.

Grateful, because it's not chemo that I'm going to get, but just an annual atomic bomb, to strengthen my bones.

I did not shake the nurse's hand and I disinfected myself with the product at the entrance.

The nurse is young.

Cheerful.

Attentive and reassuring.

He's joking with my neighbour who just coughed:

"Be careful, if you continue to cough, I'll call the hospital!"

"Ah on that, I already said to my wife on Sunday, if you call the ambulance again, I'll not be returning home!"

He tries hard to cough, to spice up his game:
"Because I'm telling you, at home, she's the boss!
"But my wife knows me well enough, she knows that if I say that I won't come back anymore, I won't!"
I venture behind the white curtain separating us:
"And ... why don't you want to go to the hospital?"
Instantly he pulls aside the sanitary white curtain and "unveils" his face to me:
I like his face.
I like faces.
I like ... the remnants of his face.
Beautiful remains, you know!
The most beautiful remains.
That have gone through life.
His life.
A unique life.
Yet I think:
"My God, it looks like he's already dead!"
The look in his eyes instantly contradicted me.
Spark of laughter.
A sucker punch to the evil little Minus.
Here, this one you will not have:
This laugh.
This insolent laugh.
Teasing.
Virile.
Mellow.
So mellow that soon it will decay.
"In hospital, they always fix you and off you go!"
He raises his old peasant arm, "de-muscled" by

the work he can no longer do.

"For four years, I have been in continuous treatment."

His eyes, however, flow with gratitude.

"I'm not whingeing, I am well cared for and I'm fine!"

He nods towards his drip:

"They all know me here and they are so nice to me!"
"Too nice Mr. N, you are unbearable!"
"Don't get smart, otherwise I will rip it all out!"

I sense he could do so, but he won't, because he's a peasant and peasants are tight-fisted.

"A fortune this treatment, so you understand, I'm not complaining.

"They just know here, I don't want to be prolonged anymore.

"If things go badly, leave me in peace!"

He looks out the window, towards the Jura, towards his mountain.

Towards his farm.

Towards his wife who's the boss ... but just at home.

"I have had a good life.

"With my wife, we have been together for 53 years."

I laugh:

"So she's a good boss!"

Spark of communion.

The evil little Minus doesn't understand anything.

Annoyed he says to himself:

"I will come back another time!"

What will happen to you my old morning companion?

Of course, if the evil little Minus catches you, it's game over!

Though…

With your fat old Jurassien peasant's head, maybe it's you who'll play a bad trick on him?

I love to think so, because …

Because your laughter still loved life!

March 13, 2020

Gathering

The Federal Council has banned gatherings of more than 100 people until the end of April.

Restaurants, bars and nightclubs can't allow in more than 50 customers.

So more than 51: "that's bad?"

But as long as you don't go over 50, you can still "go crazy!"

The main thing is that you go crazy *with finesse!*[6]

---

[6] In the original French, the word 'confinement' (isolation/lockdown) offers the pun 'con' (with) 'finement' (finesse)!

March 16, 2020

So is it serious?

I postponed my spring medical appointments.

Except the one on March 20th with my oncologist.

The doctor who knows me best.

Since 2003.

The doctor in whom I have confidence has become an accomplice.

A frail and strong woman at the same time.

She is, as for so many others who have encountered cancer, our haven.

Safe haven.

Haven of constantly updated knowledge.

Haven of maximum attention.

That form of attention so dense, that you can hold onto it physically.

Haven of serenity.

Year-round serenity subscription.

Despite the hours in the office, the evening hours at the clinic, the hours on her computer, which gives you a prescription via email, because when she gets home, she studies your analyses again.

She is…

She is my guardian angel's intimate assistant.

This Monday, March 16th, her secretary called me:

"It's the surgery, I'm calling on your doctor's behalf regarding the appointment booked for March 20th. It is not urgent, since we checked your blood on the 5th, before the Aclasta infusion."[7]

"I didn't know whether to cancel it, I didn't want to be all hysterical!"

"Not at all my God, this is very serious!

"With your medical history, do not leave your home!"

And right then, from that precise moment, Milan no longer appeared to me so far, nor China.

From right there and then, lockdown had just started for me.

With the complicity of my two guardian angels.

The one who has kept an eye on yours truly since I was born.

And the second one, with her white coat, always open and "immaculately" white.

March 18, 2020

The little Parisienne

In France, there has been a lockdown since March 17th.

Last night she called me.

From Paris.

---

[7] Medicine used to control osteoporosis

For a long time.

Facing Notre-Dame, from where she sent me the first photos, during the fire.

"I listened to an opera today ... then I said to myself, make a list of those I never call."

She chatted to me for two hours.

Commented, pictured, drew from her memories, her wounds, her dreams, her hopes.

This new love of hers, perhaps ...

A love, which like all her loves was already starting ...

Complicated.

I learned more from this than over the whole of the past 37 years.

Her work that absorbs her.

A stabilising anchor in the storms of life.

Storms that most of the time, are from gluttony loving its sensations, like others are loving their prayer-driven asceticism.

A greediness, which in its own way is a hymn to life.

This life that the little Parisienne brings to the disabled. Thanks to multiple artistic facets, which she masters with passion.

"Her disabled" who will have to stay with their families, while the evil Minus calms down.

And my disabled heart, because we always have a disabled heart when faced with love, jumped when she said to me:

For the first time in 37 years:

The little Parisienne said to me:
"I love you!"

March 20, 2020

The family business

I don't know them.
They don't know me.
But since I live opposite, I see them.
I watch them, like grandmother once observed the people of the neighbourhood.
At times I have envied them.
Two brothers. Yes, I checked the names!
In their two-storey villa, that also contains their small business.
Two brothers who live in the same house and work in the same company.
I would have so loved that ...
With you, my little brother!
A dozen employees, an apprentice.
They all seem happy to work, each in his right place.
In the weeks before Christmas the light is on all night.
It is ticking over, chugging along, working well.
In recent days, I see fewer and fewer people.
This afternoon, the young boss did everything

needed.

Emptied the bins, wrapped the packages, tied the packages up, loaded the packages, delivered the packages.

Alone…

It's Friday March 20th.

The Federal Council has prohibited gatherings of more than five people.

In our turn, we count our dead.

Far from Milan, far from China…

March 28, 2020

Under the window

In a big city in France, her father succumbed to the evil little Minus.

The family was not allowed to attend the burial.

So the funeral directors had the delicacy, to pass under her window with the hearse.

I thought, *"My God, we're in the process of replaying an old Fellini or Pasolini film!"*

And then she went to a church, empty and emptied, lit a candle.

Only an *"A-Dieu"* was tangible.

Felt.

Felt in the white wax, made in China.

The flame was not frightened.

It did not even respect the distance.

Small solitary ritual, engulfed in the infinity of pain.

No, neither Fellini, Pasolini, nor anyone else could have pictured it …

March 29, 2020

Anguish

You called me yesterday, same as every night.

Locked down in France, in your homeland, with your medical record, your doctor and … your vulnerability.

That very thing that gives your faith its authenticity.

Me in Switzerland, in my homeland, with my medical records, my doctors and … my vulnerability.

My anxious faith.

Anxious like this dread inside of me.

You're there before me:

"What scares me is to die suffocating!

"I will embrace the hit, if it happens, but not stuffed with pipes!"

I did not add:

"And me, I beg God every day that you don't die, without me being near you … "

March 31, 2020

The baby bat

Even Frankenstein will soon be overtaken.
Hitchcock a mere choirboy.
So, I'd like to tell the evil little Minus a story.
Who likes to associate himself with bats.
The story of a young girl's drama.
Well, really, that of a 29-year-old girl!
I was on holiday in Ticino.
The world was still "in order".
Enough in any case, for me to decide to do a week of tennis induction lessons.
It was quickly truncated by my orthopaedic deficiencies, the nature of which I still did not know.
So I decided to walk through the town that was in flower, since the world was "in order".
Enough, in any case, to breathe the beauty of the luxurious parks.
One day, I came across a baby bat.
Fallen from the nest?
Abandoned?
Lost on a perfectly mown lawn.
Touching.
Due to its fragility.
Its inability to fly.
Its ugliness in pitifully dragging itself across the

impeccably mown lawn.

I took it in my handkerchief and brought it back to the hotel.

A beautiful hotel, in a world still "in order".

Enough anyway to find food for a baby bat.

I fed it as well as I could, without a lot of success.

But he had brightened up and started inspecting the large dresser, moving in it more easily than on the impeccably mown lawn.

In the morning, I took it with me and put it back in its nest in the bottom of the wastepaper basket, after the cleaning lady had emptied it.

One evening I came home.

The cleaning lady had been back and re-emptied the bin. Impeccably purified.

The 29-year-old little girl started to cry…

40 years later, of course, I wouldn't cry anymore!

And then you would have blessed it.

This little creature of God.

You always bless the messes we stumble into.

Men, animals or plants.

This crazy question crossed my mind?

Should we bless the evil little Minus?

Bless our enemy?

Evil little Minus, basically, you can't help it?

It is not your fault.

You became evil because we humans, we collaborated.

Collaborated with the fallen angels.

Rushed to teach ourselves how to martyr, both

our fellow humans, animals, and the whole of nature.

Martyr Your Creation, Lord!

Your creatures.

Those which You invited us from the outset to give names to.

But yes, it was the first man who named you: "Bat!"

Funny name by the way, he could have found a better one![8]

To give a name:

To enter into communion.

With energy.

That energy that was in the Law and shouldn't have left it.

That law that we overturn with torments, to satisfy our greedy bodies.

Those that do not want to be bathed by a Lenten quarantine.

Always pushing those delicate boundaries, further away.

Until the hell of lockdown.

Until the very short hell ...

It's March 31st.

The phone just rang.

Our friend, our brother who fights tirelessly, as a nurse at the Strasbourg hospital is affected.

---

[8] In French the word for bat is *chauve-souris*, or 'bald mouse'.

His wife, fragile with lungs in panic mode.
She is the mother of four children.
How run of the mill:
There are thousands like him, like her, like them in the world, since that the little Minus decided to leave the yellow empire.
But…
They are neither in Milan, nor in China and …
Them, I love them so much more than those who fill the coffins of Milan, China or elsewhere!
It's March 31st and for the first time …
I am holding back my tears.

April 1, 2020

Saint Mary the Egyptian

Bad night.
Old somatic sores are profiting from it.
The store of usual weapons for relieving them, is depleted.
This morning I asked myself:
"What is your desire for the day?"
Reply:
"I'm recovering from my night and staying in bed for a bit."
In fact, I'd already opted for this version yesterday.

It is unimaginable that the body and the soul are fascinated by the torpor.

"Immobility is death!" thought Jean Daniel[9] who became "immobilised" a short time ago. Active centenarian until the end of the road.

I jumped out of my bed, at last a picture to kickstart my old bones! I did my physio session.

At the end of my somatic performance, I threw out my usual:

"Doxa To Theo!",[10] then I added:

"And bravo Maria!"

This wish-trap had transformed itself into a superior wellbeing.

It's April 1st.

I wonder if there will be practical jokes.

Some Swiss editorials mention "miracles at the heart of the crisis":

A federal council that governs, a population that takes responsibility, a health system that deals with the shock, thanks to the sacred union between public hospitals and private clinics...

I would have preferred us to close the borders immediately and rain down masks, but I'm just a lost citizen who chooses to trust the leaders of this country, who reassure me.

The Minister of Health, however, uses the term

---

[9] Jean Daniel (1920-2020), French writer and journalist. Founder and director of the *Nouvel Observateur*.
[10] Glory to God!

"humility".

A good segue, into reciting my prayers.

It is April 1, Feast of Saint Mary the Egyptian.[11]

Prostituted by a hunger for lust, she embarked on a pilgrimage at the age of 29, paying for her journey with her charms.

Arriving in Jerusalem in front of the Basilica of The Resurrection, a force prevented her from entering with her traveling companions.

She then turned to the icon of the Mother of God:

"I am in the mire of sin and you are the purest of virgins. Take pity on an unhappy woman and effect my salvation, that I may adore the cross of your divine Son."[12]

Soothed, she was able to enter the basilica, while a voice said to her:

"If you cross the Jordan, you will find rest!"

She lived there as a hermit for 47 years.

One day Saint Zosime of Palestine passed by. He gave her divine communion.

At her request he came by again a year later, but the saint was lying dead, her face towards Jerusalem.

With a message, begging to be buried there, where she had gone through so many battles and temptations.

But the deserted ground was so dry, that Saint

---

[11] She lived in Alexandria in the sixth century
[12] Quote from the golden legend of Jacques Voragine (Genoa 1228-1298)

Zosime could not dig her grave. Suddenly he saw a lion approaching. Saint Zosime asked him for help.

It was due to this lion, who dug with his paws, that Saint Mary the Egyptian was buried ...

It's April 1st.

I ate my breakfast, trying not to waste it, to save my reserve of provisions.

For the first time, I felt the meaning of fasting.

Beyond bodily mastery, any rite of purification.

Beyond the empty stomach, spurring on the heart to discover its emptiness in turn:

Taking care with the gift of food.

Eating it with gratitude.

Feeling the full force of the spoken grace, rather than reciting it mechanically.

To be renewed with...

The Source of Life.

It's April 1st.

Feast of Saint Mary the Egyptian.

I am convinced that if we turned ourselves back, at our own pace, with our uniqueness, our weaknesses, our darkness and our shortcomings...

If we turned back to Our Creator ...

The evil little Minus and those that move with it, will in their turn, take off to the desert. There where there are only grains of sand to invade and scorpions to infect.

Scorpions hiding under the stones when the sun crushes them. While our overly, or not-gullible-enough minds, don't know where to hide from these spillages of conflicting information that crush them.

To turn back to Our Creator is above all to turn to the Spirit of discernment, so that we men, once again kings of creation, will be able to regain control of it.

To the point of calling the lions, to bury us.

Too bad for funeral directors!

We will put them out of work.

In any case, they will have enriched themselves enough, thanks to the little Minus!

It's always April 1st.

Still no jokes.

However there's humour, when it slips in with tenderness ...

Humour is a balm!

A breath of freshness, even ephemeral.

12:30 pm:

German Swiss radio announces that Putin is sending aid to Trump to fight Minus.

Taiwan offers ten million masks to countries that lack them.

The chain of happiness has raised two million to support families who no longer have a salary.

I mock myself as I sink into the sentimentality of a signed-up senior citizen, who is in full lockdown, but I'm sure that You rejoice.

Because You are ... Compassion.

You are Compassion and You can only rejoice, that men answer You.

To hell with embittered comments, about the possible manipulated profits of one or the other.

For their revamped image.

To hell with all that saintly sniggering!

Anyway, you manage to get the Best out of it all, as soon as one of us opens up a tiny space for you.

And that is something that, the evil little Minus, he cannot do!

April 2, 2020

The tenth plague[13]

It mainly strikes our elders, although a six-month-old baby has just died in the United States.

In France there are more than 4000 dead.

Worldwide more than 46,000.

Our friend, our brother, a solid judo blackbelt, is very weak.

He who never complains, hurts.

Bone pain, back pain, pain everywhere…

It's April 2nd.

The French government is reviewing the regulations for funerals.

---

[13] Reference to the Book of Exodus 10:12

From now on, families will be able to see the deceased's face, from a good metre away.

In the photo announcing these adjustments, there was a coffin.

A flowered coffin on a rather well-mown lawn, carried by four masked men.

It was then that I thought of the tenth plague.

In a way, you could say that in recent years the planet has already counted a few:

The waters changed to "blood" ... plastic.

Frogs ... not really. Either way it would be a bargain, we would have tons of thighs to slash, to enjoy!

Mosquitoes ... yep here we are! And some have even become killers.

Flies, horseflies ... here we're doing even better, since pesticides and other chemical purifications even exterminate bees.

The death of the herds ... when the cows, which became gaga, were to be massacred en masse?

Boils ... we won with that one:

Cortisone creams, lasers, scalpels. We can even while we're at it, repair the whole phizog.

We won against the boils.

Just not yet against the evil little Minus.

He's not wasting time while he waits for us!

Hail ... included more and more in the climate change gift package.

Grasshoppers ... in Africa, but it's far away. Here it's more like ticks. Not great either.

The ninth, the one before the Minus:
Darkness[14] ...
Darkness?
What darkness?
The one in which a young girl from the North gets raised?
Who in the style of Moses[15] the stammerer stood up, to raise the flags against the pharaoh's hardened heart?
A young girl, behind whom thousands of other kids have started to run to free our planet?
And You?
You who are always present, at the time when science did not know the appropriate scissors with which to mutilate the frogs without losing too much of their miserable flesh?
You?
You who the stammerer invoked.
You who acted on behalf of the stammerer.
That stammerer You had chosen.
You?
What will YOU do when we arrive on the shores of the Red Sea?

---

[14] The darkness in the book of Exodus was the ninth plague in Egypt, before the death of the first Egyptian born for the tenth plague.

[15] Moses the deliverer of the Hebrew people, prisoner of Pharaoh in Egypt, had speech problems and made his brother Aaron speak for him.

April 3, 2020

The great Strasbourgienne

"I don't have the coronavirus.
The result is negative.
But I'm going to work.
They need me."
She attached to her message, her hospital photo.

Harnessed caregiver, she looks more like a beekeeper.

Her husband is an Orthodox priest, majoring first class in theology.

Major of combat too.

He worked for years on the shelves of Super U, to feed his family.

Then he resumed his paramedic training.

Little Minus stuck him out the way, at his patients' bedsides.

Little Minus hates majors.

Normal, when one's a minus!

This old judo blackbelt – obliging major - is in quarantine, in a studio next to his hospital.

His wife is therefore alone with their four children.

But she is not infected.

What a relief my beautiful Romanian, from a village you tell me about:

"We don't have material comfort, but we have

spiritual comfort."

Every year in summer, you send me photos:
From another world.
From another time.
You can be seen in them with your children and your characteristic candour.
Yet you are far from being the model of the balanced country girl.
With your occasional revolts.
Those that would make you get up at night, to write an outpouring to the Prime Minister.
With your sharp and honest sensitivity.
The same one that makes you regret your outbursts.
A Romanian country girl, come to do a theology degree at the University of Strasbourg.
In impeccable French.
The French with which you passed your degree in social care, because with a degree in God, we rarely have access to material comforts.
Comforts you never despise while you remain adept at simplicity.
You are pure transparency.
It oozes from your big blue eyes, hungry for love.
From the same love that carries the names of your condemned patients, through prayer.
Condemned before the Minus's arrival.
No but, he does not have exclusivity there!
Death is not his invention!
The patients who are dying and who you

accompany with your tenderness.

Your love for your family, the very comfort that is lacking in your village, has been able to leave room for the other.

This other, this stranger in a hospital bed that clings to your hand, to your care, to your eyes.

Who will perhaps have the chance to be a miracle, because The Other will have listened to your supplications.

Or who at least, will go to join Him, with the passport of your bright smile ...

It's April 3rd.

The French Prime Minister repeated yesterday that there would be no Easter holiday, no TGV, no travel.

And that the end of lockdown wouldn't be tomorrow.

Many admiring compliments, but not a word of apology for our "major at the frontline" and those who like him, fight with the only means available.

I have often wondered why a politician, from whatever party or country, could never confess:

"Here we have failed, we have not seen it coming, forgive us!"

The Holy Fathers call this approach: repentance.

The first condition for the heart to grow.

A word that startles people by suggesting self-reflection.

Who no longer choose to think in case it involves thinking deeply ...

You are at work, my great Strasbourgienne.

Quickly, with lots of hearts, flowers and kisses via your iPhone, you wrote to me:

"I love you!"

It is not the first time.

You send this regularly, without warning.

But still they have that same freshness of the evening sea breezes.

So, I hold in my tears.

I always hold them in.

I swear I hold them in, because I want them to explode with you. In your arms.

And let them burst out with our laughter.

Those we shared already.

Those we will share again…

April 4, 2020

Not me!

~Bouchons in Île-de-France, during the screening of those who were tempted to defy the ban, by going on holiday. Now they have another 35 hours, where they have to stay at home!

~A nurse who, with so many others, has twice-violated 'the 35-hour code', calls out to President Macron:

"I am not sacrificing myself; it is you who are

sacrificing me. Stop talking to caregivers as if we are good little soldiers. Soldiers have weapons. We have trash bags."[16]

It's April 4th.
~The French medical profession is divided, for or against hydroxychloroquine, prescribed by Professor Raoult[17] in Marseille.
In Algeria and in several other countries, it has started to be given systematically to all patients who test positive.
And in our brave Switzerland?
What is the news?
~26,000 additional unemployed.
Over 550 deaths.
Over 20,000 confirmed cases.
Hospitals brace themselves and wait for the wave.
It is also April 4th in Switzerland.
And here too, the cries of distress from EMS staff are being heard.[18]
Among them, a doctor from Vaud shocked that deceased patients are being replaced by new "healthy" patients, while the old ones are dropping like flies, and staff are extremely exposed. With a constant flow of cases, impossible to manage.

---

[16] Huffpost: 4.04.2020
[17] Didier Raoult, infectious disease specialist and professor of microbiology in Marseille.
[18] Ehpad correspondent in France.

I can't help being relieved that Mum and Dad are gone.

And smile about that still recent time, when the head nurse of the home told me this anecdote about Dad:

It is morning.

9.30 am.

Everyone's in the common room, breakfast finished.

The head nurse enters the room:

"Hello Mr F, it's time to go and have breakfast!"

Insomniac and used to mornings spent in recuperation, my usually polite dad answers very firmly:

"Look, I'm 90 years old, I'm in a nursing home, it's time to rest and not be pissed off!"

Point won:

He received his tray in his room.

Because this woman was trying to respect the dignity of her residents.

It was not all rosy of course, but she was far from the only one to think like that and especially to put it into practice.

It's April 4th.

Palm Saturday, Western date.

Republicain-L'Est reveals that a proportion of the masks set aside for Bourgogne-Franche Comté, that landed straight from the yellow empire at

Mulhouse airport, has been "hijacked" for the benefit of the Great East's bloodbath. ~

It's the bad news that touches me the most.

That touches me in a concrete way.

It's funny, how it changes everything:

For a banal reason: you are in Bourgogne-Franche-Comté!

And the good old egotism, so human as they rightly say, starts up.

Moreover, it gets going as soon as my eyes open in the morning.

Question number 1:

"Am I still spared?"

Question number 2:

"What about you?"

So much so that, when you call me outside the agreed hours, my first fear exclaims:

"Are you not well?"

But as far as the Great-East is concerned, with its 1,200 deaths, give or take, its exploding hospitals and exhausted caregivers, my fears can go whistle!

As can the shareholders or distant beneficiaries of the EMS, not knowing, if the fortune that room occupation costs, is covered by the healthy patients or the patients who die while suffocating!

What altruistic heart is it, in the Great East, or even the small one, or even in The East for short, that isn't above all terrorised, that his nonagenarian dad is suffocating in solitude in his Ehpad cell[19] or

---

[19] France: accommodation establishment for dependent elderly

suffocating on the hospital steps?

Because he is 90 years old, decked out with incurable ills and ultimately, if you're going to take the leap, you might as well do it right away!

With the complicity of the evil little Minus, who begins to wonder, even without meaning to, if he is carrying out the process of natural selection.

Literature offers an inexhaustible source of examples of all these passions, that have selfishness at their origin.

Or more animalistically: the survival instinct.

The most intimately heart-breaking image, is still this passage from the cult book by Elie Wiesel, "The Night",[20] in which as a child, after being protected by his father in the camps at Auschwitz and Buchenwald, the author comes face to face with him, so weakened by the vomiting of blood, he cannot even get up to go to the bathroom. From protector, he becomes a stinking burden and the anguished child, who feared more than anything, the loss of this father, comes to wish for his death.

We clearly find ourselves there, in a different register of atrociousness.

But this instinct's power resides in the lever of these reactions which horrify us, especially when we are hidden away, as in my case now:

Far from the camps.

Far from the hospital steps.

---

people, the Swiss EMS: medico-social establishment.
[20] Elie Wiesel (1928-2016)

And far from the EMS hospices[21].

Does a human being really have the capacity to reach beyond this pharaoh of selfishness, alone?

Because to be a good ecologist, king of nature, king of animals, you still have to master your instincts a bit?

"Do what you like with the Minus, so long as it doesn't reach me!

"Nor you whom I love, nor those for whom I would cry so much, such as I still am …

"I would be torn apart!"

Perhaps…

While it may not be part of the Minus's plans at all, perhaps the death knell is beginning to sound, calling him to consider crossing the desert?

The desert of our deserts.

The deserts of this awesome little screen.

So awesome, it has forgotten its core response.

Where is it, because there are questions we never ask it?

Hoping in our turn, to reach the shores of the red sea, considering ourselves to be guided, as the Pillar of Cloud and Fire[22] guided the stammerer and his people before us?

Guided by something other than our pride that only stops at our mirrors.

Dressed in the grandest of ornaments, those of our imperial freedom, we will always have a

---

[21] French Ehpads
[22] Book of Exodus 14

choice.

While on the other hand the little Minus, glorified by the black angels of terror, imposes itself dictatorially ...

It's April 4th.
Palm Sunday tomorrow, Western date[23].
Last year in Biel, I remember meeting a cheerful band of Italians, leaving their church, branches in hand.
It was last year.
Palm Sunday 2019-style.
Today, they leave cemeteries and crematoria, and still in mini groups.
The churches are closed.
It is April 4th, 2020, the eve of Palm Sunday.

April 5, 2020

Joy

I have just watched the TF2 programme "The paths of faith."[24]
The guest was the Chief Rabbi of France, Haim Korsia.

---

[23] This year 2020 the Orthodox Palm Festival will be on April 12.
[24] Every Sunday morning from 8.30am.

The Jewish Passover is beginning with closed synagogues.

This man is of a radiant tenderness which can only be contagious.

Beaten little Minus, may he catch his contagiousness, it crossed my lockdown screen!

Sublime lesson:

A lesson in spirituality embodied in the texts and their interpretation as if modelled on the current challenges.

A lesson in citizenship.

A lesson about belonging to the chosen people, not justifying this choosing by a shutting down, but by a generous openness to all the French nation, of which all claim citizenship.

To summarise his words would be to skin them, but we can enjoy them in replaying them on our screens.

Our ingenious screens.

For those who can't find the right click, I will cite only one of his sentences that has, like all the others, a flamboyant simplicity:

It is part of a theme that is dear to me:

How to turn an ordeal around:

"Joy is never in the observation that everything is fine, but in the will to be joyful."

Happy Easter, Monsieur le Grand... the very Chief Rabbi!

And with you, Happy Easter to this people, onto whom we Christians too often forget that we have

been grafted.
It's April 5th, 2020.
Palm Sunday.

April 6, 2020

Tenderness

At least 63,000 victims, since Minus got fed up with being despised in the delicious flesh of the ignoble bats, or that of the pangolins, tortured so that thanks to their scales the dicks attached to the noble flesh are less soft.

The noble flesh:

That thinks everything is allowed.

Satisfying itself with demonic superstitions, to give itself a few sparkling seconds of extra spasms.

To the point of exterminating the darling pangolin or that big black adorably grumpy bear, taking bile – alleged aphrodisiac – from him while he's alive and with no anaesthetic.

We are not going to kill a bear to get hard, right?

There are huge savings, to keeping him in a cage with a catheter!

And voilà...

Since its release into broad daylight, Minus has

already sent 63,000 noble bodies to Hades![25]

Having given them a foretaste of it in their agony.

Already weakened by age or disease, it was certainly not a case of hoping to get a better hard-on.

But this is not Minus's problem, he gets his claws into whatever he can ...

I miss my Cypriot confessor.

More than ever.

His serene step clicking across the courtyard of one of the most beautiful churches in Cyprus.

His beautiful, long beard ... impeccably coiffured.

His white bun that protrudes from his worn out koufos.[26]

Like the Chief Rabbi of yesterday, he is only tenderness.

Far from being complacent though.

Especially with himself, who at 80, imposes upon himself all the ascetic rules of the monastic tradition.

He does not miss one.

Even welcoming like an ascetic, this heat wave that made me flee at the first signs.

One day he said to me:

---

[25] Hades is equated with hell. Hades in Greek mythology is the older brother of Zeus and he reigned underground, hence the extension to the grave.
[26] Greek word. It is a kind of monk hat in light fabrics.

"God will do everything He can to bring as many people as possible into paradise!"

So, I dare to remind You of him!

Because this dear man who never hides his faith, any more than he hides his weaknesses and shortcomings, this dear ...

Your dear man proclaimed it.

He told me so in his soft voice.

With his sweet eyes.

With that sweet mischievous smile.

He told me:

Like a prayer.

Like a hope.

Like...

A certitude.

To hell with the fires of Hades!

Besides, You have been there.

From there You delivered the sinners that had been hoping for You since Adam.

This was not so as to fill it with others?

No?

I don't have the audacity to beg You.

Because...

Because I think of Your dear little man.

And if there was ever anyone, to announce this sweet hope, it was him.

So much more occupied with You than I am.

But I know...

I know that among these 63,000, or more at the time of my writing to You, there are also people there who did not even know Thy Name.

Or stupidly who did not fall in love with You, because isn't that what it's all about?

So the robe that would allow them to enter your banqueting hall,[27] can You see a little, if it concerns them?

There are even some who still have a piece of tube in their mush!

And yet they are there.

At the door.

At the door of the Feast of Your Tenderness.

Because You are Tenderness in its pure state.

So I think ...

Once again, You will not coerce them.

Logical, You would have done it a long time ago!

You will never coerce any of your creatures!

But I'm sure if they ask You to do it:

Let them be called, Jimmy, Inaya, Diego, Isaac, Assad, Esther, Liang, Daisy, Moussa, Arun, Tom...

Or even Jojo...

If they ask YOU to do it ...

You will open the door for them.

Because Tenderness:

It's YOU!

---

[27] With reference to the wedding banquet in the Gospels of Matthew (22:14) and Luke (14:15)

April 6, 2020, evening

Small gift

The deliveryman just rang, to quickly drop off my month's medication at my door.

The pharmacist had warned me that he avoided all contact.

I did not touch him.

I did not see him.

I shouted to him from behind my door:

"Thank you, good evening!"

It's April 6 ...

In my mailbox, there was also a package from Amazon, a small gift that I gave myself.

So you say to me, what is it?

Is it a book?

A spiritual book?

Guess:

Here is the title:

"Revitalift", author: L'Oréal.

Because even in the middle of Lent, and especially in lockdown Lent, my 70-year-old facade wrinkles at high speed.

It tingled a bit when I applied it, but it did me a whole lot of good.

It is April 6, the sixth week of Lent.

And fourth week of lockdown.

April 7, 2020

Boris Johnson

The English Prime Minister, infected and isolated for several days, was admitted to intensive care.

Now is not the time to find out if he'd been talking bullshit. In any case, if he has been talking it, in particular on this subject, he will have put it into practice through his recklessness.

Regardless of what results from whatever actions one or other of those in charge takes, we're all in deep shit!

Hang on Boris!

The queen, your queen made one of her rare speeches, reminding us that *"All together, we will win!"*

For once in the history of humanity, we are in one and the same boat, with a common enemy.

Let's not give Minus the extra victory of our pitiful revenge taunts!

Otherwise, it's not just a battle that we'll lose, but the war.

It's April 7th.

I just heard the caregiver, leave my neighbour's studio reassuring him:

"Don't worry, have a nice day!"

The old man is alone.

Uber alone.

More than alone.

When he approaches me, it is to grumble.

Against management, against taxes, against everything that merits complaining about.

86 years old.

Valiant.

Solid as a hundred-year-old tree.

A Juran fir.

The ones Papa wanted to see again, before he died.

"It's just my legs that no longer follow!" He grumbles again.

Yet every day, he takes his cane.

Alone.

And, without a mask, drags his big carcass, to the nearest supermarket.

I hope he will have a good day…

It's April 7th.

A French friend just emailed me.

She asks that we pray for her niece, who has just been detected positive.

A nurse, she was carrying out tests.

Without masks!

There were bread and games.

She could eat and have fun.

But there was no reserve of tests nor enough masks!

So it is certain that once we're free of this ...
Some scripts will have to be remarked.
If one wants to pass the Bac, which in Switzerland we often call:
The Maturity ...

It's April 7th.
Tuesday of The Week of Saint Lazarus.
The Patron Saint of Larnaca.
I had closed my fab little screen, to listen to an old recording from 2006, when my body still allowed me to attend all the services.
At vespers tonight we mourn his death, four days before Christ raises him.
The Christ, God and Man, who cried for His friend with our tears.
With an emotion of love not intended to be discreet.
Recalling the disembodied spirituality of the emotions that are inherent to the human heart, and which, because they were despised, psychology is now obliged to recover. Inspired by the Spirit of Science, to heal this castration. Alas, the legion of dividers, of which Minus is only a mini soldier, has often managed to cut the Word of God (Logos) from the soul (psyche). One strategy among many, to curb the complete restoration of man.
The first words that I landed upon in my recording sent shivers across my flesh:
"O Friend of the Saviour!"

Emotion again!
Indescribable emotion.
And tears.
Tears of remembrance.
Tears of gratitude.
Tears of worry.
For all my friends there, under the ever-arrogant sun.
The cathedral, My cathedral, will it be empty during this Week of Saint Lazarus?
"O Friend of the Saviour,"
Protect…
As you have done so much in the past.
Protect again, this city that is yours!
It's April 7th.
Tuesday of the week of Saint Lazarus.

April 8, 2020

A first name at night

Last night we had a "parish-video meeting".
Just to get along, looking at our more or less quarantined faces.
Nice moments of sharing.
Those which so annoy little Minus!
Dawn has not yet risen.
A rushed meal and a messed-up schedule

prevent me from going back to sleep.

So I entrust to You the name of an old friend from youth, whom little Minus massacred.

The first victim who has a different resonance for me.

Because it reminds me of a face.

It's funny as once again, it changes everything!

Statistics reveal that the majority of deaths have occurred in patients already affected by other pathologies:

Hypertension, type 2 diabetes, cancer less than five years old, chronic respiratory diseases, obesity, cardiac pathologies...

In general, it is not healthy people who succumb first.

Nothing really unexpected.

The death statistics don't at the moment appear, to be spectacularly in excess of those of the seasonal flu?

Though sufficient to force the transfer of intensive care patients to the least affected regions.

Sufficient to send out TGVs of patients who are in good health... or almost.

Some can, in this way, take a trip on the back of health & safety during lockdown.

No journalist worthy of the name will deny that he is a little, or even more than a little, on the lookout for sensationalism.

Some of our leaders, all nations combined, have revealed their inability to see ahead, as well as their weaknesses.

Perhaps even their overcapacity to boast about their army leadership skills, at war against Minus.

But from that to suspect a dictatorial plot against our democracies?

Yet he likes it, Minus!

He only saw that in hell.

His despot is the master of discord, of the spirit of disillusioned suspicion.

I do not know what pathologies my old friend, a former Olympic sportsman, had accumulated at 79 years old.

I only know that this night, pained, I pray for his soul's rest.

And...

That we remain vigilant.

Vigilant to protect our lives.

If we are indifferent to our own lives, or if we feel invincible enough to do battle with Minus, at least be vigilant to protect the lives of others.

Even those, with damaged packaging.

But vigilant also, when the time comes, to demand the final accounts balance sheet of this painful crisis with discernment. Delving into all that can remain of sincerity in the critical demands we make, without curtaining ourselves behind a bleating apathy.

It's April 8th.
"The spirit of idleness, discouragement, domination

and easy speech, move away from me!"[28] is a verse from the Orthodox Lenten prayer I recite every morning.

I don't find myself because of this more "straight in my shoes" than the rest of the world.

Let's say that these words sometimes have the advantage of making me aware of them.

Which is the first aim of these words, bandied about from year to year, often mechanically.

But they are nonetheless words, carrying energy. Bearers of a communion.

First, with all those who have recited them for centuries.

Some of whom have known how to bear fruits of holiness.

Which in effect is like having an unclean unconscious and a heart obsessed with prayer.

Communion also, with these rediscovered parishioners' faces, thanks to my fab little screen.

My little screen… onto this ugly consumerist society!

As if Dame Measure, who was so lacking in the gods of antiquity, was not also the wife of the end of the road …

It's April 8th.
Dawn has just risen.
America is on the carpet:
1943 new deaths in 24 hours.
Minus is jubilant: with this he has KO'd the first

---

[28] Prayer of Saint Ephrem the Syrian (sixth century)

world power!

He doesn't feel like himself anymore, Minus.

Making headlines and television news.

Think of it from Minus' point of view to understand, he has languished in the exquisite flesh of bats and exquisitely exciting pangolins!

It's April 8th.

Wednesday of the week of Saint Lazarus…

April 9, 2020

He will not suffer

Nature is no longer on the lookout.

She sits enthroned.

Resplendent.

Illuminated in an unpolluted sky.

Unpolluted thanks to Minus.

In the *24 Hours Vaud & Regions* newspaper for this April 9th, a cry of sincerity from the journalist Serge Michel resounds. At 80, his artist and architect father, Jean-Paul Michel, succumbed to Minus's evil deeds a week ago.

The journalist who has encountered horror during his reporting, confesses that he believed himself "hardened":

"I had had no idea that the calamity of coronavirus, that I have covered as a journalist for weeks, would hit

so close to home."

He also admits:

"I didn't think I was going to waver at the point of my father's disappearance."

A hospital emergency doctor had explained to him, that keeping him alive on artificial respiration would not get him anywhere, coating this fatal announcement with:

"He will not suffer ...

"Seeing almost all of our patients die makes us so desperate that as doctors we do everything we can to let them depart gently."

Cat got your tongue, huh Minus?

And yes, evil little Minus, you see:

There is something deep inside man that you will never manage to infect ...

It's April 9th, 2020.
Maundy Thursday, Western date.
12.30 pm.
News on *SFR 2* culture:

Another paramedic, a new yorker, vomits up his unbearable tensions.

In New York, the shimmering queen is stunned by Minus, patients are languishing in overcrowded waiting rooms, emergency cases are arriving, already dead ...

More news on sexuality.

Sexuality in the Covid 19 Period.

Covid 19, I recall, is the official name of Minus,

and that rather pleases him, because it was the top brains that named him that.

It doesn't mean that he'll spare them in return.

Sexuality therefore struggles to adapt to the new normal:

~Unemployed prostitutes

~Those who, as a bonus, risk catching AIDS, because on that front controls are relaxed, all being centred on Minus

~The closure of brothels and sex shops

~Increase in private sex parties

~And...

Safety.

Safety, more than ever in being faithful to his or her partner~

Something that cheers certain fanatical Polish clergymen, according to the news of the day, still calling Minus "divine punishment" against the sin of homosexuality, pornography and other lusts for delighting humanity, who had been waiting for Minus to treat us all.

With that who won't go missing in the revolt of the hearts of young and old alike, in the face of a God who whispered in the moment of his own agony, the most unfair that history has ever known:

"Father, forgive them for they know not what they do!"[29]

In this world ~ which certainly often flouted and even tortured creation, and its creatures, even this

---

[29] Luke 23:34

wonder of the human body ~ one can nonetheless wonder, if it is the opportune moment to recall the platitude that all trials are "permitted by God" for our holiness?

By omitting that The Son of God addressed the Pharisees with these words of targeted clarity:

"... Hypocrites! Because you are closing the kingdom of heaven to men; you do not enter it yourself, and you do not let those who want to enter!"[30]

Nevertheless it is bound to be that among these great orgies, or less big or even mini orgies, there are some who wish to enter the kingdom of heaven?

But that is another subject...

April 10, 2020

Containment fulfilled

Puff of joy this Good Friday morning, Western date:

Not only is my great Strasbourgienne negative, but her chief priest is recovering.

Minus lost the match!

The news reveals that President Macron, on an unexpected visit to Marseille, spent three hours

---

[30] Matthew 23:13

with Professor Raoult.[31]

Never too late to meet the wise elders, even the less wise, in the field.

It matters little that they appear to be cowboys, in a crisis that no one can boast of having seen coming.

Nor of managing it, without wading through what must be called an inevitable chaos of cacophonic contradictions.

The radios, the TV channels and my iPhone balance information that verifies and denies, according to the discoveries that all hope for.

Fortunately, there are also plenty of tips for a successful lockdown:

~Cookery recipes which are a challenge for me, because I suck at them.

~How to hold on to your muscular buttocks during quarantine.

With this one, I am downright captivated, especially since mine were not so before.

~How to be stronger psychologically, since it is well known:

"Everything that doesn't kill me makes me stronger."[32]

~How to become zen, how to invent a lockdown sexuality, how to be entertained, how to manage your schedules, how to avoid your dog getting infected, how not to gain weight?

---

[31] Op. Cit. 14
[32] Nietzsche

Yes, because our lockdown fridges, I'm thinking now of mine, are crammed full. So it's really important that I don't come out of quarantine. Because, even if there are finally masks for everyone, I won't be able to hide the pounds on my belly!

Unless…

Unless Minus has reminded us that there is something else…

Something, beyond this obsession with appearance?

The one that made me buy Revitalift…

We hear plenty of interviews with famous and unknown people. Like this gentleman yesterday who said that at the beginning, it had been difficult, despite the beautiful garden, that he had available to him and his family.

~What to do with all this time?

~How to occupy the children?

~How to busy yourself?

~How to fill this time, that had been stolen by a stressed life for such a long time?

Then this father explained that by the second week, time had stolen itself back.

Delicious lockdown period transfigured into joy.

Quite simply, the joy of being together.

Reinventing connections, games, activities, laughter and pleasure. Those that life at 300 km/hour had left at the edge of the highway.

To use the current phrase:

Getting back your 'me time'.

He doesn't like all of that much, Minus.

These family reunions.

He isn't the affectionate type, Minus.

In addition he lost his match against a major.

It's no good.

I, also, really want to increase his anxiety further, with a word he can't stand.

No doubt the bitterness, which I'm assured Revitalift is slowing down with spectacular effects.

I really have to take revenge in my own way.

Because...

There's a word that I'm missing.

If I'm missing it, it's because I lack it.

Or ... because I am lacking it?[33]

It's the word: compassion.

Because beyond my wrinkled forehead, my too-many kilos, those recipes I messed up again, that garden that I had but, so long ago, that balcony that I no longer have, that family in paradise that I won't be seeing again anytime soon. Well, as long as Minus does not get involved ...

Beyond the reserves of my freezer and beyond my ingenious little screen:

There are men and women.

Who are suffering.

---

[33] These 3 lines and the 2 final lines play upon the fact that the French for 'I miss xyz' is literally 'xyz is missing to me'. The nuance/word play does not work at all in English!

Who are dying or who are mourning those that Minus has killed.

Those who might not have died so quickly ...

"Have compassion for all beings, rich and poor; everyone has their suffering. Some suffer too much, others too little."[34]

The wisdom of Buddha's phrase has more resonance than ever before.

Coinciding with the nobility of a Good Friday.

This Good Friday 2020, where alas, we will no longer be able to take a spin on the roads.

All time's highways.

So many escapes to this memory from a long time ago, that the One who liked to call himself "The Son of Man", restored Time.

By letting himself be raised on the wood of taunts…

Out of compassion!

So this Friday, April 10, Friday of the week of Saint Lazarus, before going to see, what I am going to get out of my fridge, I have decided to add to my prayer:

"Give me compassion!"

The thing I'm missing.

The thing ... that I lack!

---

[34] Buddha

April 11, 2020

Snags

New York.
The splendid.
The powerful.
The vain sometimes ... sinks into the apocalypse.
More than 2000 slain in one day.

Horrifying scenes, of refrigerated trucks supplying mass graves, with corpses wrapped in plastic bags.

My iPad...
Another awesome one, who manages through the jungle of news, to transmit the world to me.

The world outside my studio lockdown.

This kindly mini screen, it too, has displayed a provocative ad:

"How do sex addicts manage during lockdown?"

Explanations that the psychiatrist Jean-Victor White has agreed to deliver to the, at least evocatively named, "Vice" website.[35] Jean-Michel Blanc is a bipolar disorder psychiatrist, a specialist in new addictions at the Saint Antoine hospital in Paris and teacher at the Sorbonne. He strives in his research, but also in his educational communications to the general public, to change perceptions of mental illness.

---

[35] Vice Media, developed around the "Vice" magazine in 1994.

Which by the way, never amounts to imposing it as a norm, against all ontological essence, in the name of "Holy Pseudo Liberation!"

His report on sex addicts during this ongoing lockdown, the patients he lets speak, and his comments, are as edifying as they are upsetting.

Authentic.

Clear.

Instructive.

Because sometimes, in order to mimic tolerance or rush into the liberating breach of forgiveness, it is good to understand.

At least to try.

Thank you young psychiatrist sir, pop culture psychoanalyst too, thank you for transmitting this demonstration to us, the pure and the less pure.

Too often we forget that the original meaning of sin is that of:

"Missing your goal", "aiming badly", "aiming to the side".

Now these "vicious ones" are all testifying to this "failed shot".

Today's great revelation regarding their demons made me think of the great saint after whom, Dr Blanc, your hospital is named. I am thinking more specifically of the one, prior to Saint Anthony of Padua:

Saint Anthony the Great.[36]

---

[36] Third century in the desert of Egypt, considered the father of monasticism.

Founder of Christian hermitism, he is famous for his power in combatting demons.

The demons' faces may have changed. They adapt too!

But their sagacity in enslaving, degrading and torturing men is no less effective.

So from the bottom of my studio quarantine, I have the audacity to make two wishes:

The first, dear Doctor Blanc, is that your patients invoke the great ascetic, a brother to us all, to help them.

I swear he is waiting for that!

The second is that the disciples of Saint Anthony remember their master's battles. Not only to drool over beautiful hymns on his feast day, but also to have a compassionate prayer for all those who are facing demons.

The demons of all time.

Perhaps, following the example of the true holy ascetics, to even give each of them a boost, for flushing out their own demons?

Basically, everyone is a winner.

Except...

Minus.

I'm sure it would be a huge blow to Minus and all his friends!

It is April 11, Holy Saturday 2020, western date. And for us, Saturday of the Resurrection of Lazarus.[37]

---

[37] For Orthodox Christians in this year 2020.

April 12, 2020

Happy Easter

More and more photos of my childhood appear on my social networks.

So many adorable baby faces.

From fresh colours, large eyes filled with wonder, promising smiles. The very best, of what the photographers of the time, were allowed to draw out from these cherubim.

Who sometimes, regardless of Rousseau's[38] treatises on man being born naturally good, can from the cradle show signs of selfishness, jealousy or even manipulation.

But these faces, our faces are touching.

It was before.

Before life dents us.

Even reinforcing itself with assault tanks, to crush some of us.

I then thought of the famous "sin of Adam ".

Children dented from generation to generation, by parents dented from generation to generation, themselves dented by their parents from generation to generation.

As if there was a lack of maturity from the very beginning.

A damned contagious immaturity.

---

[38] Geneva writer and philosopher (1712-1778)

A wound that will have to be endured, or at best accompanied, from generation to generation.

This wound etched on each of our faces:

Would it not be worthwhile to try to decipher the message?

Before Minus or another of his generation takes it?

It's April 12.

Western Easter.

The Queen of England, who was driving ambulances under WWII bombs, said yesterday that darkness and death had never been victorious. And that we had to look to the future with the hope of Easter light.

In the Christian Orthodox tradition, the lockdown Holy Week begins tomorrow.

It is therefore our Palm Sunday this April 12th.

April 13, 2020

Agitation

For the first time, on this Great Monday of our Holy Week 2020, while protecting myself as much as possible from the omnipresent alarms, I had a burst of agitation:

"Will it really last until the end of the year?

"*Or more?*"

On all the websites selling protective masks: nothing. Absolutely nothing.

This suggests that our leaders' advice on their ineffectiveness has not been heard.

Out of stock.

So I ordered fabric and rubber bands.

The concern being I am a seamstress of unparalleled incompetence and clumsiness ...

It's April 13.

Discharged from hospital, Boris Johnson is recovering. A miss there, Minus!

Ruffled, he thanked with emotion those who saved his life.

Gratitude is a gift.

The next step from that is a downright grace:

That of having come close to death and come out of it with the oil of humility.

The future will tell us, if Boris brought a bottle back with him…

April 14, 2020

Drought

The drought got even worse in Switzerland, over the Easter weekend, where temperatures are already at summer levels...

According to the WHO, Covid 19, AKA little Minus, is ten times more deadly than the H1N1 flu.

A little short of two million confirmed cases in the world.

Five hundred thousand cured.

Almost 130,000 deaths, including approximately 16,000 in France and 1,200 in Switzerland.

Figures which do not all lead to the same scenario:

In Ecuador, no refrigerated trucks, or even mass graves. The Vice President has made apologies for a government that is completely overwhelmed:

Corpses rot in the streets, in the courtyards of houses, on the pavements. For the better off, in a big box.

If only bodies dried up as quickly as hearts.

In Nigeria, the most populous country in Africa where Christians have once again become martyrs, the curfew has been decreed.

Street markets are destroyed by mechanical shovels or burned. A young man exclaims into the microphone of a BBC World journalist:[39]

"It is not the virus that will kill us, but starvation!" More than ever, the "world's forgotten beggars" are painting hell.

Dantesque hell on the colossal fresco of so-called "modern" times.

---

[39] BBC World, Monday 13.4.20, news from Africa

There is the distress of the wealthy, worried about getting an appointment with their shrink quickly, to manage post lockdown.

And there is the distress of the wretched, the lousy "damned".

The distress that will not cure our tears!

Nor avoid some of us rushing into even more poverty and despair because of Minus!

What if the girl with her flags, like so many hypersensitive antennae, had simply captured the echo of our collective unconscious silence?

It is 14th April, our Great Holy Tuesday 2020.

April 15, 2020

Plague

Another difficult night.

My carcass needs even more disciplined care, to avoid trouble.

It misses the outdoors, walking, swimming.

Commonplace, I must not be the only one ...

The postman rang below to bring me a tracked parcel:

"Wait, I'm coming down!"

"No, I'm leaving the package here Madame, have a nice day!"

I could not hold back this whisper deep inside of

me:

"I don't have the plague!"

Yet I was relieved.

Despite my attraction to faces, I was relieved not to meet his.

Him too.

Given the state of mine, despite the Revitalift, it's not his loss!

Bravely continuing to do his job, allowing me along with so many others, to cope with this isolation better.

It's April 15, 2020.

The Great Holy Wednesday.

For a few days now, I have been trying to remember the beautiful songs I loved so much in the Cathedral in Paris.

Often the words come back to me, the melodies too, but incomplete.

So I launch into them and …

An advantage of isolating, I don't damage any ears:

"Illuminate the robe of my soul, O Giver of Light…"[40]

It is the Great Holy Wednesday 2020.

---

[40] Tropaire (liturgical poem) sung at the Matins of this Great Wednesday.

April 16, 2020

Maundy Thursday 2020

The translators of my German and English books have just sent me my latest work.

A modern tale in which I also write of hope.[41]

Even before the arrival of Minus.

On the cover, I put the photo of a squirrel.

Today I feel a little out of step with my squirrel.

Yet she reminds me that life has been, is and always will be, filled with delight and lightness.

It also reminds me that I will have to get to work:

Proofreading and corrections.

This unique solitude provides a good setting.

But first...

I'm going to find my icons and my attempts and bad singing.

It's Great Thursday.

The Great Thursday, where, in a society from a long time ago ...

One that didn't know of our greed for consumerism, one of Yours was found, who was sufficiently greedy and avaricious, to deliver You up for thirty coins.

---

[41] See appendix

April 17, 2020

Good Friday

Still in his stunning masterpiece "The Night", Elie Wiesel[42] recounts one of the most terrifying scenes in all of autobiographical literature:

Inmates of the Auschwitz camp had to march past the hanged men, looking them straight in the face. One day among the condemned inmates, a twelve-year-old child, too light to die immediately, agonised horrifically for more than half an hour:

"He was still alive, when I passed him ... Behind me I heard [an inmate] ask: "Where then is God? And I felt a voice inside me answering him: "Where is he? - He is here: he is hanging on this gallows..."[43]

This child, Your child, did not accept it freely.

However, he is no less a martyr for that.

Martyr of a prize for revolting, for this freedom that You allow to even the most perverse of demons!

However...

Elie Wiesel was right:

God, *"Where is he?*

Here he is, he's hanged..."

It is Good Friday 2020.

In a society that doesn't seem to have been better

---

[42] Nobel Peace Prize 1986
[43] The Night, 1958

than ours, a long time ago:

"The Son of Man" was hanged on the wood of the cross.

It was the first Good Friday.

April 18, 2020

Holy Saturday 2020

If Minus hadn't got his passport, issued by customs to the less cautious among us, this morning I'd be celebrating Holy Saturday in my cathedral in Larnaca.

Where the quarantined priest, his acolyte and his cantor, celebrate the Holy Week of 2020, behind closed doors.

After the liturgy, at Vespers, there is a rite of striking intensity:

The Descent of Christ into Hell, to snatch back the prisoners who had been there since... Adam.

The rites have this specificity of meaning, whatever the holiness or the mediocrity of those who are celebrating them, to spring up from the depths of centuries. And to engrave, not only in our souls, but also in our flesh, symbols which are bridges.

~Bridges to those who have continued the rites from the depths of these centuries

~Bridges to those who continue to celebrate them, far beyond the walls of my dear cathedral

~Bridges to this more or less watered garden…

This garden deep in our hearts, which one day received a breath.

A breath that it neither explained, nor understood, nor even wished to retain… -

It is Holy Saturday 2020.

How many times have I neglected to water you, this corner of my heart, to retain Your Breath there?

Fortunately, You don't count them!

So You, who came down to snatch Adam up from hell, go down into that of my heart!

Have mercy on me! And…

"Take pity on this world which is Yours!"[44]

April 19, 2020

Orthodox Easter Sunday

More than 20 years ago, when I spent Easter in Cyprus in its rough form still, I remember that the morning after the night of The Resurrection, I went to the small fishing port. Nobody was working there, but the fishermen dressed in their Sunday

---

[44] Holy Saturday morning service stanza.

best were talking in groups. At this time, bathed in intact tradition, they all greeted each other with the words:

"*Christ is risen!*" And the answer to this greeting was:

"*Verily, He is risen!*"

It was a true pacifying joy that I've never since felt elsewhere.

Thank you my old friends, many of whom are in heaven.

Thank you for sharing this transmission which was almost innate to you.

It will have a place, along with all your faces burned with sun, salt and wind, brightly tender at the bottom of my heart...

It's Sunday April 19.

In Mulhouse, we are slowly starting to dismantle the military hospital, which was set up during the disaster.

A doctor from Limoges, after offering to help this dramatically stricken region, returned home and testified. Not only to the crossing of hell, but especially to the incredible commitment of all the nursing staff. Inventive, on duty continuously, united and ready for anything to fight you Minus!

All different shapes, ages, origins and colours, united and welded.

There Minus, you will have lost points! Many points that mean the game will not turn in your favour.

So many of these beautiful starred points, that it should start to discourage you!

The Queen was right, darkness and death were never victorious.

It is Sunday April 19, Sunday of Easter Light.

Monday April 20, 2020

My heroes of the day

Of course, these hundreds of thousands of health workers around the world, need to be at the top of the list.

These fighters, with their two feet, two hands and two eyes in the dirt.

But on this bright Monday[45] I myself, clueless about science, wished to pay tribute to "my" heroes of the day:

These scientists or entrepreneurs who one day had the energy, to make real a genius intuition. Thanks to them, I can open my small screen and above all, I can share.

Share with my nearest and dearest, those less close, and even with those I'm not close to at all. Get

---

[45] Bright or bright Monday, so we call the days of the Orthodox Radiant Week, after Easter.

out of my isolation, my grumbles, my micro-universe.

As the dangers of brainwashing and addiction are recognised, I don't care to go through them.

Nothing new:

With atomic energy we can light up or burn up our entire planet.

Isn't life a permanent danger?

Even while it's a permanent miracle?

It's up to us to take care of ourselves, when the alarm bells sound.

It is up to us to refrain from constantly imitating that good old Adam, impatient to grab all the knowledge for himself, before progressing a little in his ripening.

Thank you, thank you to all of you who opened these doors to me.

First of all my dear brother Laurent, who gave me my first computer lessons when I was in the middle of radiotherapy sessions.

But also you, at first reluctant about these techniques, who offered me those courses in Bordeaux, at our lovely Isabelle's home.

Who knew how to convince you to take the leap, to introduce you to this world which became familiar to you, to the point of having "co-celebrated" with your young colleagues, via a repeat broadcast.

Who would have thought that the Spirit would slip into these little devices one day?

Who would have thought that one day we would be crying watching replays of the release of Agios Phos[46] from the tomb in Jerusalem?

You can't believe it Minus, huh?

You're still a bit confused there, right?

Among these explorers, I would like to remember the inventor, at age nineteen, of the calculator: that has a name that reminds me of a dear friend: Pascaline.

Pascaline, named after Blaise Pascal.[47]

But maths and I share no connection at all.

It is above all Pascal's mystical experience that attracts me.

The one which, from November 1654 pushed him to devote his thoughts solely to philosophy and theology.

However, despite being able to honour his famous "night of fire",[48] I am less adept with this famous phrase from "Memorial":[49]

"God of Abraham, God of Isaac, God of Jacob, not philosophers and scholars ... "

Although referring to the learned philosophers

---

[46] The Holy Light which has miraculously sprung for generations. from the Tomb of Christ in Jerusalem for the Orthodox Easter.

[47] French mathematician, physicist, inventor, philosopher, moralist and theologian (1623-1662).

[48] Night from 23 to 24 November 1654, night of the conversion of Blaise Pascal.

[49] Written on this fiery night, the night of 23 to 24 November 1654.

called Cartesian, whose intellectual deduction opposes mystical experience, rather than offering synergy with it, this "attack" is legitimate.

Especially since, alas, the "modernised" man persists in this rupture. With his dry intellect that shrivels him, forcing a disconnect with his heart. That drowns him, by dint of barricading him against any form of verb.

But what captivates me is this intuition that infuses a scientist, an artist or a creator.

As if at some point, the angel of invention opened a box?

Most of the time, by the way, in a brain that has dug, dug and dug again, accepting mistakes with exemplary humility.

Neurons, the unimaginable circuits of our fabulous brain, some would say.

Based on scientifically proven research. Equally precious barriers to the full powers of a diabolic obscurantism, that often lurks throughout history on pious church benches, and whose only obsession has been to make people forget that the Spirit of Science is also a gift from God.

Just like Minus and his gang, the sole aim being to sow chaos up to the very border of "Intelligence", dividing, stultifying and paralysing the famous free will.

Faith worthy of the name worships the Spirit of Science.

Oh that the angels, friends of neurons, choose to

slip themselves into small boxes and to be opened one beautiful day or beautiful night ...

So You who blow everywhere, far beyond the borders of our churches, those of religions or non-religions,

You:

When are You going to send an angel with the box that contains the remedy against Minus?

I dare to ask You, because I know despite my heroes of the day and of science ...

Of Your Science…

I know You can!

Of course, if You are waiting until we all turn to You, I can put a notice online.

It won't be the first time.

Nor the first time I pass for a crazy old woman!

It's April 20, bright Monday 2020.

April 22, 2020

Other big tears

~Two and a half million cases reported worldwide

~Nearly seven hundred thousand cured

~About one hundred and eighty thousand deaths

Here is today's assessment of your pandemic,

Minus! I would like to curb your enthusiasm:

This pandemic also reveals that at the bottom of man, there is an icon of dedication, solidarity and compassion.

It is clear that you and your clique, you master subtle tricks, to strangle these virtues.

But there my dear, you begin to collect failures!

So if I were you, I would go back to the boss, before you lose the advantage!

It's April 22

This morning after my physiotherapy session, I once again felt how beneficial the movements of the body are.

Beneficial also for the friends of the angels, the neurons.

As Doctor Frédéric Saldmann[50] reports, who I quote in one of my books:[51]

"...Finnish scientists have shown that daily physical exercise, made us make new neurons every day."

And at any age too, which never fails to encourage me ...

It's April 22

On the radio, I listened to Verdi's famous "Nabucco."[52] I saw myself again as a child, when

---

[50] "Your health without risk" Dr. Fréderic Saldmann
[51] "Illness, My Complicit Enemy" Maria Andreas
[52] Opera by Guiseppe Verdi (1841) with the famous: "Va pensiero" or song of the Hebrews (in captivity in Babylon under king

my parents, musicians, introduced us to this opera every weekend.

Dad mimicking the conductor.

A memory of great tenderness, even if the wounds of the Hebrew choir were a bit like those of our hearts, at times rebellious or already prisoners…

It's April 22.

One last piece of news that will seem almost trivial:

This time an alarm cry from the elephant carers, in Thailand's parks. In the absence of tourists, the pachyderms are threatened with famine.

I know Minus, as long as it hurts, you are delighted to add elephants to your trophies!

You have never even watched an elephant that's crying! Because elephants, they mourn!

Big tears…

Very big elephant tears …

April 23, 2020

Corona coup

18 years ago on 23rd April 2002 the surgeon was

Nebuchadnezzar in -586 BC.)

beaming after the lymph node biopsy. Announcing that despite our worst fears, there were no metastases in the lymph nodes.

It was the feast of Saint George 2002.

Today to celebrate, I engaged in a bit of a corona coup:

I took out the age-old scissors and I cut the rest of the hair that remained on my head.

At the back it's as uneven as a Russian mountain range, but from the front it reminds me with affection, of the cut my grandfather gave me, calling me afterwards: *"My little Joseph"!*[53]

It will be noted that this is not yet, despite the equality of the sexes, a female first name ...

April 24, 2020

Freedom

Paul Eluard[54] in the occupied Paris of 1942, wrote:

"On my desk and the trees
On the sand on the snow
I write your name…

---

[53] In reference to Joseph of the Old Testament, son of Jacob.
[54] Paul Eluard (1895-1952) French poet, belonging to the movement of surrealism.

...
On the health returned
On the risk vanished
On the hope without memory
I write your name
And by the power of a word
I start my life over
I was born to know you
To name you.
Freedom."

Obviously I miss writing on the sand.

Singing in the sea and laughing with you!

I had a painful somatic day yesterday, a worrying hint that the body is still getting weaker inside these four walls.

Yet more than ever I experience ...

I feel ...

And...

I check my freedom!

Without panicking, I realise that time is "running out".

I see moreover, that my days of lockdown are passing by at lightning speed.

So beyond the wants and desires, there arises an emergency to hang on to the golden thread.

To the Golden Thread.

And to the Golden Son![55]

---

[55] Wordplay in the French original: thread "fil" and son "fils".

This Golden Son ...

This Royal Son, He Alone who can give me my true Freedom.

First and foremost, because He is the One who gives to me, but never, never, never asks for anything back:

"Why don't you comment on the brilliant article I sent you?"

"Why haven't you signed this vital petition yet?"

"Why don't you share my anger, my rebellion, my 'woke' decision, my actions, my carefully aimed sarcasm or my hours of online prayer?"

He offers it me, without the slightest gesture of impatience.

He offers it me ... ready if I wish, to embellish it.

Embellish it in truth.

His Truth.

Which is none other than this, to not hurt the other and to love him, him too with his procession of freedoms:

Unique.

Intimate.

Sacred.

"The human being is in the image of God and therefore potentially has the capacity for freedom deep in his software, in his hard drive."[56]

This is why I too:

---

[56] Father Marc-Antoine Costa de Beauregard, conference on "the wounded words of Christianity", 1.7.2018: the word "Church", orthodoxie.com.

Freedom…
I wanted to write your name.

April 26, 2020

Nostalgia

Everything is always better in the past, so with our noses buried in it, we aspire to a more promising future.

But there are pictures that warrant our contemplation, like those landscapes of Oberägeri posted on "Facebook", by one of my former students.[57]

The boarding school clinging to the hill opposite the lake and the mountains, with the Alps in the distance.

Nature still chaste, just a few houses. But so few, that nothing could have stopped the car of a distracted colleague, who without speed and without handbrake, could have bumped through one field after another, to the village!

To this series of photos, from which a much more purified light than that "imposed" by Minus spreads, a comment from another world was added:

---

[57] In the canton of Zug in Switzerland.

"Don't forget the Sunday letter!"

Every Sunday, there was the ritual of the "Sonntagsbrief",[58] which pupils had to write to their parents, and which were collected by the principal, whom we called "the chief".

From these photos and this sober and soberly tender comment, emerges a breath of paradise.

I don't want to find other words:

Except remember that of gratitude.

It's Sunday 26th April.

On these fields which awaited the passage of the seasons:

Villas, blocks ... padded out.

It is development and it is what it is.

Besides, nobody if it was offered to them on a plate, would refuse a luxury apartment. At least not me!

I just hope that those who are facing the lake, the mountains and the congested valley, still stop, as I stopped on leaving work, to breathe.

Or stop breathing…

In front of the beauty of creation!

---

[58] Sunday letter

April 27, 2020

Some numbers

Figures that are a long way off those of the Spanish flu, reassure the media. Some claim that they are not even worse than those of the seasonal flu.

Nearly two hundred and six thousand dead worldwide.

We are bordering on three million infected.

In Switzerland more than twenty-nine thousand tested positive and more than one thousand three hundred died.

As for the statistics of more deaths or fewer deaths than on this date last year, they are raining in from all sides. With diverse rivalling comments, ranging from the fear that poor people are being walloped the hardest, to cheers for the flawless management of the authorities. Each will take a view, according to his or her standpoints, which also rival each other in their diversity!

In France, 'progressive deconfinement', a wryly amusing term, is planned for May 11.

In Switzerland we started today: The hairdressers are taken by storm.

Garden centres and DIY stores too:

The never-ending queues in their car parks, that they have had to close between the assault of two hordes.

It's almost moving:

This garden awaiting its fertilizers and seeds.

Those that grandmother, snuffed out by Minus will no longer see grow, but she was 93 years old, a good age, so flowers, she'd seen enough.

This closet better suited for the kids' room, which we will be able to paint with them.

And if we still have money, we will buy a home cinema with a giant screen, so that we will be less bored by the next Covid wave.

You see Minus, we have resources, even if one of your accomplices shows up after your defeat!

"Let me see my own faults and not judge my brother!"

That's an even more essential trick than the bags of fertilizer, the paint, the sofas suited to a home cinema, to enjoy almost-live crimes and enjoy those golden landscapes where we will never get to go because grandmother's legacy was too meagre, and we had to share it with the others!

The others who have already been there, although they complain all the time!

But hey, it's family and family is sacred!

Sofas on which to enjoy those frozen pizzas, which we will pile up in the new freezer that we will get tomorrow quickly while it's on offer, too bad if we spend the whole morning queueing again.

Sofas to enjoy… in short! The least short possible however, so as not to not to have to torture a bear or a pangolin at exorbitant prices!

At least the economy will recover and our children and grandchildren will no longer be unemployed! Phew!

"Let me see my faults ... "

These words of Lent have returned to the closet that I would like to change, but I do not have the strength to tinker with it.

Home cinema, I don't have room. Neither for the sofa.

As for the freezer, mine is already clogging up my kitchenette and I often wondered, during this lockdown intended to reconnect me to the Essential, where I could put it.

It is 27th April, my first outing in town or rather, my first round-trip in town.

The rain will come at last.
Tomorrow I will go out by breathing through my mask, the raindrops and snail smell that I loved when I was a child.

Others will come out, then others and still others.

Others will never go out.

Never again.

And you will have to get used to not seeing them on the street or in the garden.

Others will be infected.

Others will be cured.

There will be new quarrels over numbers, statistics, what should have been done, what has not been done, but what will be done by others.

There will be calls for a global awareness, so many demands from this maturity that Father Adam lacked!

One day we will find a remedy.

A vaccine.

And your time will come Minus!

Mine too, by the way!

And You?

You?

You are ...

Still there?

Still patient?

Patient with Your obsessive respect for our freedom?

So before that day ...

Before my day comes, I dare to remind You:

Even if I forget again.

Even if I prefer to let myself be carried away by the serene hymn of the rain.

Of Your rain.

Even if the great lent has passed, I dare to ask You again:

"Let me not judge my brother!" And even less, by *"loose talk"*:

That stranger whose heart I never met ...

May 28, 2020

Epilogue

America exceeds 100,000 dead.

But that country has gone through so many hardships since its creation.

Starting with that of shedding its blood so that enslaved men could again be free.

Minus did not succeed, despite his treachery and will never manage to shackle freedom.

Europe, for its part, has also passed the 100,000 dead mark.

Figures that mean little, until one of our loved ones is taken away.

However infections are falling fast and from deconfinement to deconfinement, we will soon be able to regain our freedom. Finally, that of our somatic mobility. The other remains an independent conquest of Minus and his clique.

In France, places of worship are opened again. We celebrate there with masks, "purifying our hands" at the entrance.

Other countries like Brazil are in the middle of a fight.

And You?

Today, among Orthodox Christians, the feast of Your Ascension is being celebrated.

We are taught that You raised our human

nature, fallen and glorified thanks to Your Passion, with the Father.

And that from there, You will send the Holy Spirit to us from the Father, to fortify us.

To fortify, what can that mean when we are constantly buffeted left, right and centre?

I have no other suggestion than that it means to continue…

To continue with this fragility which makes man moving.

So moving that You will never forget him!

END.

May 28, 2020, Feast of the Ascension among Orthodox Christians.

Postscript 1
March 4, 2021

One year on

Nature is trampling.
Lightly.
On the lookout, ready to catch fire at the sun's slightest provocation.
And he, the little Minus?
Nanometer so light in nature[59].

Him? He didn't even gain weight, despite gorging himself on more than 2.5 million corpses[60] in the past year!

Statistics again!

Statistics that annoy, continue to frighten, repulse, render indifferent, are accepted as official

---

[59] At the start of this journal, March 4th 2020
[60] More than 115 million infected, approximately 90.3 million cured. Figures from https://fr.statista.com/themes/6050/le-coronavirus-covid-19 01.03.2021

or rejected as fake!

One of the points scored by Minus, unfortunately:

Division, suspicion, accusations, even insults towards those who have forcibly taken the wrong decisions, or are complicit in a gigantic plot, destined to enslave us.

As if we ourselves weren't enough, each of us standing by our own bullshit ...

Whereas Minus had not yet reached my small provincial town last year, on this date, it has now reached the whole world. And with it our entire economy, our lifestyles, our freedoms, our privacy ...

Shortness of breath, fatigue, fedupness, or the despair of those who have lost everything, continue to rub shoulders with a form of recklessness, but no one is truly spared.

Once again, poor countries are crushed more than others. While our tabloids and tv media zoom in on the anger of those who are frustrated over a good coffee, on a sunny terrace. This is normal, once again:

It's human...

Overcoming one's own suffering is the privilege of the saints, regardless of the faith that engendered them.

Since the end of 2020, different vaccines have been administered, as never before in history.

You just got your second dose, and I'm so

relieved, grateful ...

While waiting for my turn, I am preparing, like last year, to receive my atomic bomb against osteoporosis.

I continue to trust the Spirit of Science, and those who dedicate their lives to it ...

Obviously, there is disagreement with the vaccines, which is to be expected.

Future treatments are being tested ...

We hope for the end of the tunnel ...

I want, even though I have known moments of rebellion, anguish, doubt and exhaustion, to only hold on to those moments of victory:

First on a large scale:

Thousands of exhausted men and women have sacrificed themselves all over the world day and night to heal others.

Some, despite the restrictions, have invented stratagems with maximum security, so that patients in a coma, can hear the voices of their loved ones, or feel their hand on theirs, before leaving.[61]

In some French suburbs, young Muslims embodied their faith, visiting and feeding the isolated and quarantined elders.

But also Christians, Jews, atheists, so much solidarity that you almost lost the meaning of your mission, Minus!

What I missed the most, what I still miss the

---

[61] For example at Bordeaux University Hospital, under Professor Denis Malvy.

most - like so many others – is, the sharing:

Face to face, eye to eye ...

When will I finally be able to hold in my arms my great Strasbourgienne or my Cypriot sister?

We had to hold on. We must hold on…

So I muddled through somehow, continuing to "create":

To write…

To rewrite my "modern tale" about teens[62], complete it[63] and even create an online store of T-shirts and accessories, with designs drawn directly from this tale.[64]

It wouldn't have been possible without my colleague, Jacqueline and her team[65].

In the prison imposed by Minus, I have never worked so hard. Every day, we exchanged, laughed, exposed our differences, our expectations, our impatience.

Did you not expect that, Minus?

And I'm sure we're not the only ones, so I'll give you a tip: Go back to where you came from!

Because This Seal of Life, This Smile of Tenderness in the depths of man, you will never get to grab it away ...

---

[62] *I Tell You Never Give Up* Amazon 2021)
[63] *Raphaela's 24-Hour Detox*
[64] www.mariaandreas.eu: 'Gab & Co. Designs'
[65] www.hugejam.com

Postscript 2
October 26, 2022

You took your revenge Minus!

You and your clique. Your sub-clique rather, because with the days, weeks, months, years, you too have aged and you are running out of steam!

But you got me stranded anyway, and I've been drooling for three weeks!

My friend, translator and editor of my English books, Jacqueline[59], got her share too. After spending a wonderful day and evening in London for a Robbie Williams concert. It was the birthday present her son had given her. So you weren't going to miss the chance to catch her! She is so the opposite of your bunch of destroyers. Another one of those stupid idiots who respects the value of family, work, friendship, authentic sharing. In the electric night that connected her to her idol and all

---

[59] www.hugejam.com

his fans, you were waiting for her! Two days later she was not AOK, even though her vaccinations, her age and her constitution allowed her to withstand you. We regretted not being able to heal together to try to get a few bursts of laughter out of it. By pursuing the projects of a crazy young and a crazy old woman who still believe in a better world. A world where all together, we would unite our efforts to get rid of your posse that continues to weaken the weakest. Have you nothing new to tell me? The weak are there to be weakened!

To clear the way...

To leave room for the race of the strong! Those who do not know the weight of a damaged carcass, a deficient immune system or simply the weight of years. Those who are strong in their heads too, in their minds, in their intact instincts, in their splendid psychic and emotional balance!

Those who really have the faith! Because deep down they know that they are so much the chosen ones, that they risk nothing but being saved!

It's true that with us, you had an easier job, right?

We doubt, we tremble, we pick up our rubbish and our wounds every morning to try to move forward. We still haven't managed to tame this emotional depth that gnaws at us with each tremor, with each anxious thought, with each of these doubts, that divert us or bring us closer to our creator. This life that we have instinctively placed above our salvation. Not that it appears so, of course! Because there one can rest assured, Bible or rosary in hand. Top notch hearts!

Vaccinated three times, just before what I continue to consider one of the miracles of science, my fourth vaccine, I got away with it like millions of other infected people.[60] However, with the panoply of those symptoms that I do not even wish on those who continue to call Covid a myth. A myth assembled from scratch to knock us off our feet. Suffocate me and those with me who are unaware that vile beings are using every means to terrorise us. To paralyse us in order to – and this is something quite new – make gigantic profits by lining their pockets! Not to mention that we remain unwitting puppets of the huge plot that will lead us straight to the apocalypse! It's funny by the way, because in the debility of my little enslaved conscience, I have not yet lost the certainty that this one, this final Apocalypse, will be decided by the Boss as to the day and the hour! You know what, while a fratricidal war is on our doorstep with the exploited and delightful spectre of a possible nuclear war, which would thus make this apocalypse almost instantaneous, I bathe once again in one of my blissful contradictions! That of persisting in believing that it is the Boss who will decide!

---

[60] At the end of this October there will have been 628M infected and 6.53M dead.

Unless...

Unless the Boss ends up getting fed up!

Fed up with our witch hunts, with our intolerances that drool with pride, fed up with seeing these kids or their grandfathers blessed, before being shredded by the cannons. Beautiful cannons, moreover, that we show off with the arrogance of our omnipotence! The very one that you, Minus, with your clique, laughed at, because you defeated it, before it could cry out! Fed up with our selfishness, our constant suspicions! Fed up with our holy freedom to consider that being a man and a woman at the same time opens a new path to liberation! Fed up with our democracy so liberated that it fired the boss! Fired at from every corner of our superb and successful lives so that we are stuffed with sleeping pills, anti-depressants or drugs. Not to mention these so-called social networks, spilling the news of the most cursed disasters that, alas, only an informed elite is able to discern! Hey about drugs, I tried CBD oil to calm my nights of non-stop coughing and it's not bad. Especially since though I write pretty texts about prayer and about my fellow monks, I can't manage, even inwardly, to get out two words of my so comforting heartfelt prayer[61] when I'm constantly gasping all over the place! Another nice slap down to your humility my daughter...

But back to the Boss!

---

[61] Lord Jesus Christ, Son of God, have mercy on me.

To the Good Master...

To whether He had decided to abandon us to our endless bullshit?

I remember one remark – among many – from my dear mother a few months before her death:

"Darling, do you know why God didn't forgive Adam?"

"No my dear maman, why?"

"Because he would have started again...

Without limits!"

As for my good dose of flu, Minus, you managed to target one of my weak points, my bronchial tubes![62] Can you imagine having smoked for the best 15 years of your life and worked for 25 years with year-round bronchitis, all in the flower – by the way, a very beautiful flower – of age! You remember it all along, Minus, and tadah you hook yourself to it!

Frankly Minus, hats off to you, I'm having a great time!

To the point where, more than three weeks after my positive PCR, I'm not able to go to Cyprus and take my Cypriot family a copy of the book that I have just had published[63], about my most beautiful love story, my story with that island! The one that

---

[62] Unfortunately, I was unable to obtain the famous Paxlovid recommended at the first symptoms by my wonderful friend, Professor Denis Malvy from Bordeaux, or simply Father Denis to me, since he is also a priest. The perfect marriage of high level science and even higher level Science!

[63] *Cyprus, I Have Embraced Your Heart*, Huge Jam, 2022

tourists don't see...

The Island of All Saints!

Among them there is one that I particularly like:

Saint Lazarus, the patron saint of Larnaca.

So... You know what I did Minus?

In the depths of my night, my face smashed with insomnia, cortisone inhalations and medication of all kinds, homeopathic, natural or less natural, I have just postponed my flight to a day that I have chosen especially:

November 8, feast of the powerful celestials, synaxis of the holy archangels Michael, Gabriel and Raphael who are the protagonists of my children's novel: I Tell You Never Give Up.[64]

Never give up!

Even though I failed... because I was no longer myself. An old piece of shit who felt less shit one morning, when my niece Mireille came to place behind my door the perfect anti-depression hamper. It was then that the tissues, the toilet paper, the chocolate, the honey, the organic fruit and above all the large portion of pumpkin soup cooked with art, comforted me more than any incantation of my filthy heart!

However...

If God allows...

Soon...

On one of those blessed November evenings in Larnaca, I will walk along the promenade by the

---

[64] To be published next...

sea. I will taste the wind even though it carries that dust that I know well. The avenue will be crowded. More and more cars. Their sound smothering that of the waves...

And I will fork off just before the castle.

I will see it immediately!

Standing for centuries...

Unprovoked by those imposing cathedrals that get lost in wanting to embrace the heavens.

Just its sleek beauty.

God it is beautiful. God it is divine! God it is God in the autumn twilight...

The two side doors will be open, letting in the evening breeze. Straight from my best ally, the sea.

I will place myself a few metres from his great reliquary after having kissed his relics... through the mask that I will continue to wear in this very crowded place, because I do not want you to eat me a second time Minus, nor one of your recent acolytes!

Yet at this hour of vespers we will only be the few regulars! The old women of the neighbourhood who have nothing else to do but attend vespers...

Vespers a few metres from Saint Lazarus...

I will pray to you, St. Lazarus, for my old friend that Minus slew. That adorable old man who anointed me when I dragged my crutches, my cervical collar, my cancer or my tears to offices after the departure of those I loved so much! I will remember each of these tears, welded forever to these stones, to these sublime icons, in this sand where so many candles have oozed. So many flames of supplications, hopes and ex-votos that have joined those of all these faithful, like me more or less unfaithful, who have venerated you for centuries...

You, the Boss's Friend![65]

I know that once again I will cry...

But it will be tears that you, Minus, will continue to ignore otherwise you would instantly cease your machinations. Yet those tears have already overcome you, and if I cannot leave in November, I will leave at Easter.

And you will see those tears!

Tears that love life.

Tears that love my life more than anything.

Tears.

My tears.

Those of my love and gratitude...

FIN.

---

[65] St. Lazarus was a beloved friend of Jesus.

Books by Maria Andreas

Illness, My Complicit Enemy - Amazon, 2018

Arthritis, Osteoporosis, Breast Cancer and Other Scourges - Amazon 2019

Sparkles of Intensity - Huge Jam 2020

The Tenth Plague - Huge Jam 2021

Raphaela's 24-Hour Detox - Huge Jam 2021

Hook Up with Your Angel - Huge Jam 2022

Cyprus, I Have Embraced Your Heart - Huge Jam 2022

Cyprus, Your Heart, Your History - Huge Jam 2022

I Tell You Never Give Up - Huge Jam 2023

Maria Andreas

BORN IN ALGERIA, with Swiss/French dual-nationality, Maria Andreas sat her baccalaureate at La Chaux-de-Fonds, in French-speaking Switzerland. She then travelled for two years across Asia and Africa in a campervan. After studying modern languages (Zürich, Cambridge), she worked for 25 years as a French teacher in German-speaking Switzerland. Then she moved to Bordeaux and resumed studies in orthodox theology (Paris) and applied psychology (Düsseldorf). During this time she engaged in a long analysis with Professor Gérard Ostermann, in Bordeaux. During a one-year stay in Cyprus, she fell in love with the Greek language and the spirituality of Orthodox monasteries. It was then that she returned to her writing which, as a high school student, had already earned her first prize in Strasbourg's 1967 European Essay competition.

www.mariaandreas.eu

www.ingramcontent.com/pod-product-compliance
Lightning Source LLC
Chambersburg PA
CBHW050302120526
44590CB00016B/2455